The language of friendship is not
words, but meanings. It is an
intelligence above language.

Henry David Thoreau

Other books in the *"Language of" Series...*

Blue Mountain Arts®

It's Great to Have a Brother like You

It's Great to Have a Sister like You

The Language of Brides

The Language of Courage and Inner Strength

The Language of Happiness

The Language of Love

The Language of Marriage

The Language of Parenting

The Language of Positive Thinking

The Language of Prayer

The Language of Recovery

The Language of Success

The Language of Teaching

The Language of Teenagers

Thoughts to Share with a Wonderful Daughter

Thoughts to Share with a Wonderful Father

Thoughts to Share with a Wonderful Mother

Thoughts to Share with a Wonderful Son

You Will Always Have an Angel Watching Over You

The Language of
FRIENDSHIP

A Blue Mountain Arts® Collection
Edited by Susan Polis Schutz

Blue Mountain Press™
SPS Studios, Inc., Boulder, Colorado

Library of Congress Catalog Card Number: 98-42695
ISBN: 0-88396-479-1

ACKNOWLEDGMENTS appear on page 48.

Certain trademarks are used under license.

Manufactured in Thailand
Sixth Printing: October 2001

 This book is printed on recycled paper.

Library of Congress Cataloging-in-Publication Data

The language of friendship / edited by Susan Polis Schutz.

    p.   cm.
   ISBN 0-88396-479-1 (alk. paper)
   1. Friendship—Literary collections. I. Schutz, Susan Polis.
PN6071.F7L36 1999
177'.62—dc21

98-42695

CIP

SPS Studios, Inc.

P.O. Box 4549, Boulder, Colorado 80306

Contents

(Authors listed in order of first appearance)

Friends Are Special Treasures

Friends enlarge our world. They make us feel important and more secure in life. Friends work together. They create magic together. They help each other. They get busy, but they keep each other in the forefront of their minds and in the recesses of their hearts. Even when they're apart, friends hear each other's thoughts. Their influence on each other makes a lasting impression.

Friends cross all barriers of race, creed, age, gender, and country to connect only with the heart and spirit, which have no walls. Sometimes they don't even know it when they say the right words at just the right time. Sometimes friends <u>feel</u> <u>like</u> family. Sometimes they <u>are</u> family.

The soul hungers for friendship, someone to associate with, to compare stories with, to go places with, and to call on the phone. We keep the gift and get the blessing of friendship by passing it on to others in this give-and-take world. Thank you for this gift. What a blessing you've been to me!

Donna Fargo

When I have opened my heart to a friend,
I am more myself than ever.

 Thomas Moore

Don't walk in front of me
I may not follow
Don't walk behind me
I may not lead
Walk beside me
And just be my friend.

Albert Camus

All men have their frailties, and whoever looks for a friend without imperfections will never find what he seeks.

So long as we love, we serve. So long as we are loved by others, I would almost say we are indispensable; and no man is useless while he has a friend.

We are all travellers in the wilderness of this world, and the best that we find in our travels is an honest friend.

— Robert Louis Stevenson

What Is a Friend?

What is a friend? I will tell you ✦ It is a person with whom you dare to be yourself ✦ Your soul can be naked with him ✦ He seems to ask of you to put on nothing, only to be what you are ✦ He does not want you to be better or worse ✦ When you are with him, you feel as a prisoner feels who has been declared innocent ✦ You do not have to be on your guard ✦ You can say what you think, so long as it is genuinely you ✦ He understands those contradictions in your nature that lead others to misjudge you ✦ With him you breathe freely ✦ You can avow your little vanities and envies and hates and vicious sparks, your meannesses and absurdities and, in opening them up to him, they are lost, dissolved on the white ocean of his loyalty ✦ He understands ✦

You do not have to be careful ❧ You can abuse him, neglect him, tolerate him ❧ Best of all, you can keep still with him ❧ It makes no matter ❧ He likes you — he is like fire that purges to the bone ❧ He understands ❧ He understands ❧ You can weep with him, sing with him, laugh with him, pray with him ❧ Through it all — and underneath — he sees, knows and loves you ❧ A friend? What is a friend? Just one, I repeat, with whom you dare to be yourself ❧

 C. Raymond Beran

The only way to have a friend is to be one.

A friend may well be reckoned
the masterpiece of nature.

A friend is a person with whom I may be
sincere. Before him, I may think aloud.

— Ralph Waldo Emerson

A true friend is somebody who can make us do what we can.

God evidently does not intend us all to be rich, or powerful, or great, but He does intend us all to be friends.

— Ralph Waldo Emerson

There are plenty of acquaintances in the world, but very few real friends.

You can hardly make a friend in a year, but you can lose one in an hour.

— Chinese Proverbs

Have no friends not equal to yourself.

There are three friendships which are advantageous, and three which are injurious Friendship with the upright; friendship with the sincere; and friendship with the man of much observation; these are advantageous Friendship with the man of specious airs; friendship with the insinuatingly soft; and friendship with the glib-tongued; these are injurious.

— Confucius

Though I am different from you,
We were born involved in one another.

 Tau Ch'ien

A faithful friend is a sturdy shelter
He that has found one
Has found a treasure.

 Ecclesiasticus 6:14

Love your neighbor as yourself.

 Leviticus 19:18 (NKJV)

A friendless man is like a left hand without a right.

Hebrew Proverb

Two are better than one, because they have a good reward for their labor. For if they fall, one will lift up his companion. But woe to him who is alone when he falls, for he has no one to help him up.... Though one may be overpowered by another, two can withstand him. And a threefold cord is not quickly broken.

 Ecclesiastes 4:9-10, 12 (NKJV)

A friend is one
to whom one may pour
out all the contents
of one's heart,
chaff and grain together
knowing that the
gentlest of hands
will take and sift it,
keep what is worth keeping
and with a breath of kindness
blow the rest away.

 Arabian Proverb

Friendship is, strictly speaking, reciprocal benevolence, which inclines each party to be solicitous for the welfare of the other as for his own. This equality of affection is created and preserved by a similarity of disposition and manners.

True friendship between two people is infinite and immortal.

— Plato

He who throws away a friend is as bad as he who throws away his life.

 Sophocles

Instead of herds of oxen, endeavor
to assemble flocks of friends about
your house.

 Epictetus

One of the most beautiful qualities
of true friendship is to understand and
to be understood.

 Seneca

If a man could mount to Heaven and survey the mighty universe, his admiration of its beauties would be much diminished unless he had a friend to share in his pleasure.

Friendship renders prosperity more brilliant, while it lightens adversity by sharing it and making its burden common.

Never injure a friend, even in jest.

— Cicero

❧ Friendship Is... ❧

Someone who is concerned with everything you do • someone to call upon during good and bad times • someone who understands whatever you do • someone who tells you the truth about yourself • someone who knows what you are going through at all times •

Someone who does not compete with you
someone who is genuinely happy for you
when things go well   someone who tries to
cheer you up when things don't go well
someone who is an extension of yourself
without which you are not complete

Susan Polis Schutz

❧ Friendship Is... ❧

...fruit gathered from trees planted in the rich soil of love, and nurtured with tender care and understanding.

Alma L. Weixelbaum

...a present you give yourself.

Robert Louis Stevenson

...like a star that guides the way, near and far.

Catherine Plumb

...the only cement that will ever hold the world together.

Woodrow Wilson

...forgetting what one gives, and remembering what one receives.

Dumas the Younger

...the inexpressible comfort of feeling safe
with a person having neither to weigh
thoughts nor measure words.

George Eliot

...a reward from the past,
an enrichment of the present,
and a legacy for the future.

 Judith J. Yerman

...one soul in two bodies.

Pythagoras

...the spiritual inspiration that comes to
one when he discovers that someone else
believes in him and is willing to trust him.

 Ralph Waldo Emerson

To have a friend is to have one of the sweetest gifts; to be a friend is to experience a solemn and tender education of soul from day to day. A friend remembers us when we have forgotten ourselves. A friend may praise us and we are not embarrassed. He takes loving heed of our work, our health, our aims, our plans. He may rebuke us and we are not angry. If he is silent, we understand. It takes a great soul to be a friend.... One must forgive much, forget much, forbear much. It costs time, affection, strength, patience, love. Sometimes a man must lay down his life for his friends. There is no true friendship without self-sacrifice. We will be slow to make friends, but having once made them, neither life nor death, misunderstanding, distance nor doubt must ever come between.

 Anonymous

i am so glad and very
merely my fourth will cure
the laziest self of weary
the hugest sea of shore

so far your nearness reaches
a lucky fifth of you
turns people into eachs
and cowards into grow

our can'ts were born to happen
our mosts have died in more
our twentieth will open
wide a wide open door

we are so both and oneful
night cannot be so sky
sky cannot be so sunful
i am through you so i

 E. E. Cummings

The greatest of delights
and the best of joys
is to know that
    people like to
    be with you,
and to know that
    you like to be
    close to them.

 Maxim Gorky

To be true friends,
you must be
    sure of one another.

Leo Tolstoy

The world is so empty if one thinks
only of mountains, rivers, and cities;
but to know someone who thinks and
feels with us, and who, though distant
is close to us in spirit, this makes the
earth for us an inhabited garden.

Johann Wolfgang von Goethe

It is chance that makes brothers
but hearts that make friends.

Von Geibel

The Arrow and the Song

I shot an arrow into the air,
It fell to earth, I knew not where;
For, so swiftly it flew, the sight
Could not follow it in its flight.

I breathed a song into the air,
It fell to earth, I knew not where;
For who has sight so keen and strong,
That it can follow the flight of song?

Long, long afterward, in an oak
I found the arrow, still unbroke;
And the song, from beginning to end,
I found again in the heart of a friend.

 Henry Wadsworth Longfellow

Let us be what we are and speak
what we think and in all things keep
ourselves loyal to truth and the
sacred professions of friendship.

Henry Wadsworth Longfellow

A slender acquaintance with the world
must convince every man that actions,
not words, are the true criterion of the
attachment of friends; and that the most
liberal profession of good-will is very far
from being the surest mark of it.

 George Washington

There Is No Friend like an Old Friend

There is no friend like an old friend
Who has shared our morning days.
No greeting like his welcome,
No homage like his praise.

 — Oliver Wendell Holmes

The better part of one's life
consists of his friendships.

 Abraham Lincoln

New Friends and Old Friends

Make new friends, but keep the old;
Those are silver, these are gold.
New-made friendships, like new wine,
Age will mellow and refine.
Friendships that have stood the test
Time and change — are surely best;
Brow may wrinkle, hair grow gray;
Friendship never knows decay.
For 'mid old friends, tried and true,
Once more we reach and youth renew
But old friends, alas! may die;
New friends must their place supply
Cherish friendships in your breast
New is good, but old is best;
Make new friends, but keep the old;
Those are silver, these are gold.

 Joseph Parry

The more we love, the better we are;
and the greater our friendships are,
the dearer we are to God.

By friendship you mean the greatest love,
the greatest usefulness, the most open
communication, the noblest sufferings, the
severest truth, the heartiest counsel, and
the greatest union of minds of which brave
men and women are capable.

— Jeremy Taylor

Take Time

Take time for friendship when you can.
The hours fly swiftly, and the need
That presses on your fellowman
May fade away at equal speed
And you may sigh before the end
That you have failed to play the friend.

Not all life's pride is born of fame;
Not all the joy from work is won.
Too late we hang our heads in shame,
Remembering good we could have done;
Too late we wish that we had stayed
To comfort those who called for aid.

Take time to do the little things
Which leave the satisfactory thought,
When other joys have taken wings,
That we have labored as we ought;
That in a world where all contend,
We often stopped to be a friend.

Edgar A. Guest

I Saw in Louisiana a Live-Oak Growing

I saw in Louisiana a live-oak growing,
All alone stood it and the moss hung down from the branches,
Without any companion it grew there uttering joyous
    leaves of dark green,
And its look, rude, unbending, lusty, made me think of myself,
But I wonder'd how it could utter joyous leaves standing alone
    there without its friend near, for I knew I could not,
And I broke off a twig with a certain number of leaves
    upon it, and twined around it a little moss,
And brought it away, and I have placed it in sight in my room,
It is not needed to remind me as of my own dear friends,
(For I believe lately I think of little else than of them,)
Yet it remains to me a curious token, it makes me think of manly love;
For all that, and though the live-oak glistens there
    in Louisiana solitary in a wide flat space,
Uttering joyous leaves all its life without a friend a lover near,
I know very well I could not.

                                     Walt Whitman

Blessed are they who have the gift of making friends, for it is one of God's best gifts. It involves many things, but above all, the power of going out of one's self, and appreciating whatever is noble and loving in another.

If you have a friend worth loving,
Love him, yes, and let him know
That you love him ere life's evening
Tinge his brow with sunset glow;
Why should good words ne'er be said
Of a friend till he is dead?

— Thomas Hughes

You know how I feel
You listen to how I think
You understand...
You're
my
friend

There is no need for an outpouring
of words to explain oneself to a friend
Friends understand each other's thoughts
even before they are spoken

— Susan Polis Schutz

I haven't seen you in a while
yet I often imagine
all your expressions

I haven't spoken to you recently
but many times
I hear your thoughts

Good friends must not always be together
It is the feeling of oneness when distant
that proves a lasting friendship

— Susan Polis Schutz

I Love You

I love you,
Not only for what you are
But for what I am
When I am with you.

    I love you
    Not only for what
    You have made of yourself
    But for what
    You are making of me.

I love you
For the part of me
That you bring out;
I love you
For putting your hand
Into my heaped-up heart
And passing over
All the foolish, weak things
That you can't help
Dimly seeing there,
And for drawing out
Into the light
All the beautiful belongings
That no one else had looked
Quite far enough to find.

I love you because you
Are helping me to make
Of the lumber of my life
Not a tavern
But a temple;
Out of works
Of my every day
Not a reproach
But a song.

I love you
Because you have done
More than any creed
Could have done
To make me good,
And more than any fate
Could have done
To make me happy.

You have done it
Without a touch,
Without a word,
Without a sign.

You have done it
By being yourself.
Perhaps that is what
Being a friend means,
After all.

 Roy Croft

W hat do we live for, if it is not
to make life less difficult to others.

 George Eliot

I have perceived that to be with
those I like is enough.

 Walt Whitman

If I can stop one heart from breaking,
I shall not live in vain;
If I can ease one life the aching,
Or cool one pain,
Or help one fainting robin
Unto his nest again,
I shall not live in vain.

 Emily Dickinson

If we build on a sure foundation in
friendship, we must love our friends for
their sakes rather than for our own.

Charlotte Brontë

Be true to your word,
your work, and your friend.

As I love nature, as I love
singing birds, and gleaming
stubble, and flowing rivers, and
morning and evening, and summer
and winter, I love thee my friend.

We do not wish for friends to
feed and clothe our bodies —
neighbors are kind enough for
that — but to do the like office
for our spirits.

— Henry David Thoreau

The most I can do for my friend
is simply to be his friend.

Think of the importance of friendship in the
education of men. It will make a man honest;
it will make him a hero; it will make him a saint.
It is the state of the just dealing with the just,
the magnanimous with the magnanimous, the
sincere with the sincere, man with man.

The language of friendship is not words, but
meanings. It is an intelligence above language.

— Henry David Thoreau

True Friendship
Has Many Ingredients

True friendship isn't seen
    with the eyes;
it's felt with the heart
when there is trust,
    understanding, secrets,
loyalty, and sharing.
Friendship is a feeling
    rarely found in life,
but when it is found
it has a profound impact
    on one's well-being,
strength, and character.

A true friendship does not need
    elaborate gifts
or spectacular events
in order to be valuable or valued.

To ensure long-lasting quality
    and satisfaction,
a friendship only needs
    certain key ingredients:
undying loyalty,
unmatched understanding,
unsurpassed trust,
deep and soulful secrets,
and endless sharing.
These ingredients, mixed with
personality and a sense of humor,
can make friendship
last a lifetime.

 Sonya Williams

ACKNOWLEDGMENTS

We gratefully acknowledge the permission granted by the following authors, publishers, and authors' representatives to reprint poems or excerpts from their publications.

PrimaDonna Entertainment Corp. for "Friends Are Special Treasures" by Donna Fargo. Copyright © 1996 by PrimaDonna Entertainment Corp. All rights reserved. Reprinted by permission.

HarperCollins Publishers, Inc. for "When I have opened my heart..." from SOUL MATES by Thomas Moore. Copyright © 1994 by Thomas Moore. All rights reserved. Reprinted by permission.

Liveright Publishing Corp. for "i am so glad and very," copyright © 1940, 1968, 1991 by the Trustees for the E. E. Cummings Trust, from COMPLETE POEMS 1904-1962 by E. E. Cummings, edited by George J. Firmage. All rights reserved. Reprinted by permission.

Regnery Publishing, Inc. for "Take Time" from COLLECTED VERSE by Edgar A. Guest. Copyright © 1934 by Regnery Publishing. All rights reserved. Reprinted by special permission of Regnery Publishing, Inc., Washington, D.C.

A careful effort has been made to trace the ownership of poems and excerpts used in this anthology in order to obtain permission to reprint copyrighted materials and give proper credit to the copyright owners. If any error or omission has occurred, it is completely inadvertent, and we would like to make corrections in future editions provided that written notification is made to the publisher:

SPS STUDIOS, INC., P.O. Box 4549, Boulder, Colorado 80306.

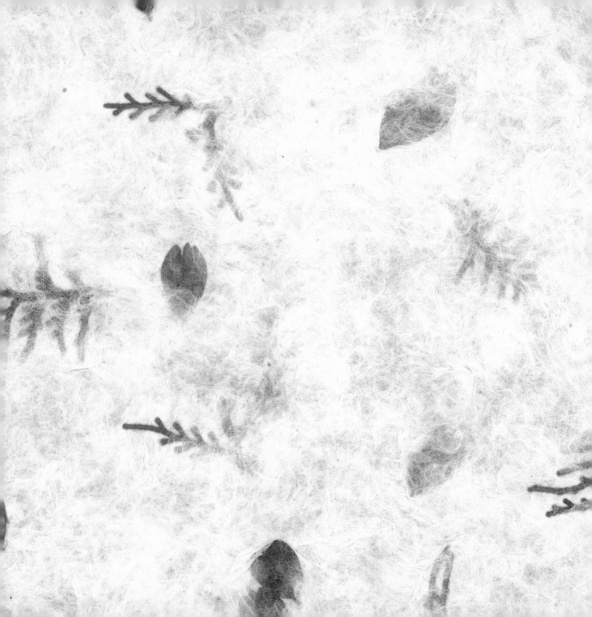